Surviving the
Shadow Pandemic:

The Mental Health
Implications of COVID-19

Surviving the Shadow Pandemic: The Mental Health Implications of COVID-19

Authors

Austin Mardon, Catherine Mardon, Lydia Sochan, Sara Djeddi, Ann Ping, Vedanshi Vala, Omar Abdul Hadi, Michaela Dowling, Romina Tabesh, Joylen Kingsley, Lilian Yeung, Shannon Lin

GM

PRESS

First Printing: 2021

Cover Design and typeset by Clare Dalton

Chapter title font: Accanthis ADF Std

(Copyright © Arkandis Digital Foundry
under the GNU General Public License V2)

ISBN 978-1-77369-664-5

E-book ISBN 978-1-77369-665-2

Golden Meteorite Press

103 11919 82 St NW

Edmonton, AB T5B 2W3

www.goldenmeteoritepress.com

Contents

Chapter 1:

The Mental Health Implications
of
Social Distancing

Sara Djeddi

Introduction

The severe acute respiratory coronavirus 2 (SARS-CoV-2), causing the COVID-19 disease, was first identified in China in December 2019 (Marroquín et al., 2020). On January 30th, 2020 it was announced by the World Health Organization (WHO) that COVID-19 was a Public Health Emergency of International Concern (Tull et al., 2020). Shortly after, on March 11th, it was officially declared a global pandemic by the WHO. In addition, "due to COVID-19's long incubation period, ease of transmission, high mortality rate (relative to the seasonal flu), and lack of pharmacological interventions, governments have had to implement extraordinary physical distancing interventions to slow the spread of the virus" (Tull et al., 2020, p. 1). In terms of public health, these separative intervention methods are effective in reducing the transmission of the COVID-19 disease (Tull et al., 2020). On the contrary, despite their physical health benefits, social distancing measures, as well as stay-at-home orders, can be economically and socially disadvantageous (Tull et al., 2020).

Studies have suggested that the negative outcomes of these interventions could result in psychological consequences such as increased loneliness, reduced social support, depression, anxiety, and financial concerns (Tull et al., 2020). Specifically, quarantine, which is complete isolation to prevent the spread of an illness, is associated with psychological distress such as depression, generalized anxiety disorder (GAD), insomnia, and post-traumatic stress (Marroquín et al., 2020). The orders from government officials to stay at home can impact the daily life of individuals, causing them to believe there is a higher risk of their physical, social, and financial health being negatively impacted, which in turn leads to an increase in anxiety and financial stress (Tull et al., 2020). These separative interventions are also a tremendous change to the social life of most individuals (Tull et al., 2020). The limited contact with their social circles can result in unwanted feelings, such as loneliness and isolation (Tull et al., 2020). Consequently, it is crucial to determine and examine the mental health implications of the social distancing measures in place (Marroquín et al., 2020). Despite the fact that there is limited research on the psychological consequences of COVID-19, previous widespread diseases proved to have consistent outcomes (Tull et al., 2020). For instance, the 2003 SARS epidemic was associated with a 31.2% rate of depression and a 28.9% rate of anxiety, both of which are significant (Tull et al., 2020). Similarly, the 2009 H1N1 pandemic was linked to high levels of anxiety (Tull et al., 2020).

The Impact of Social Distancing on Mental Disorders in the United States

A study involving a large online sample of adults from the United States was conducted in March of 2020, when the pandemic had begun to accelerate (Marroquín et al., 2020). The research focused on the implications of social distancing on individuals, specifically its symptomatic connection to depression, generalized anxiety disorder (GAD), intrusive thoughts, insomnia, and acute stress, all of which result from negative or stressful events (Marroquín et al., 2020). Essentially, the research investigated the relationship between mental health, social distancing measures, and social resources in the beginning stages of the COVID-19 pandemic (Marroquín et al., 2020).

The social distancing measures mentioned accounted for two levels, both private and public (Marroquín et al., 2020). The public measures are essentially referring to the stay at home order, or the lockdown, enforced by government officials (Marroquín et al., 2020). At the time, it was prohibited to leave the house for reasons other than essential purposes such as grocery shopping (Marroquín et al., 2020). In terms of the private level, individuals also practice 'personal distancing' in order to decrease the COVID-19 rate of transmission, such as staying a distance from those that are non-household members (Marroquín et al., 2020). Using various methods of measuring mental health effects, the impact of social distancing on the aforementioned Americans was determined (Marroquín et al., 2020). It was found that both distancing levels were linked to symptoms of mental health conditions, such as depression (Marroquín et al., 2020).

The manner in which individuals react to stressful circumstances is partially attributed to their social resources (Marroquín et al., 2020). Unfortunately, the health interventions needed for the COVID-19 pandemic have a negative impact on the social factors promoting good mental health (Marroquín et al., 2020). These processes include social support availability, day-to-day interaction, and social influences on coping, which impact mental health in a positive manner (Marroquín et al., 2020). These protective resources are important when facing psychological struggles, such as this pandemic (Marroquín et al., 2020). Moreover, one of the researchers' goals was to determine whether or not the use of these resources can mitigate the negative implications of the social distancing measures
(Marroquín et al., 2020).

The aforementioned social resources refer to both social network size and social support in current relationships (Marroquín et al., 2020). Regardless of the helpful social resources, the public and private levels of social distancing measures independently demonstrated an increase in the symptoms of the mental health disorders (Marroquín et al., 2020). The two streams of processes were included in the study in order to discuss social distancing from a different perspective, including other social factors affecting mental health (Marroquín et al., 2020). However, despite the addition of social resources known to aid in mental health, it was concluded that they are not enough to disregard or eliminate the implications of social distancing (Marroquín et al., 2020).

As previously stated, this specific study discussed the impact of the social distancing measures on the symptoms of depression, generalized anxiety disorder (GAD), intrusive thoughts, insomnia, and acute stress (Marroquín et al., 2020). Regardless of the social resources present, the researchers anticipated that the magnitude of the symptoms accompanied by these mental disorders would increase with both private and public social distancing (Marroquín et al., 2020). Depression and GAD are both mental illnesses that are commonly seen as a result of exposure to stress, which would be the pandemic and its intervention measures in this case (Marroquín et al., 2020). The researchers measured depressive symptoms by asking participants to use a scale from 0 to 3 based on the frequency of these symptoms (Marroquín et al., 2020). Similarly for GAD, participants rated how often they felt worried, nervous, and anxious on a scale from 0 to 3 (Marroquín et al., 2020). Intrusive thoughts are characterized by unwanted anxious and stressful thoughts, and can be associated with various other disorders such as obsessive-compulsive disorder (OCD) (Marroquín et al., 2020). In this case, participants rated their COVID-19 related intrusive thoughts over the period of one day on a scale from 0 to 4 (Marroquín et al., 2020). Insomnia is a disorder that is associated with sleep difficulties such as difficulty falling asleep, and a scale from 0 to 4 was used (Marroquín et al., 2020). The last psychological disorder discussed was acute stress, which is stress overload after a traumatic event (Marroquín et al., 2020). Individuals scored their stress level within the period of a week from 1 to 5 (Marroquín et al., 2020).

With the nationwide sample of adults used, it was determined that public and private social distancing measures were associated with symptoms of depression, GAD, intrusive thoughts, insomnia, and acute stress (Marroquín et al., 2020). In addition, personal or private social distancing was linked to greater levels of depression, GAD, acute stress, and intrusive thoughts compared to public measures (Marroquín et al., 2020). As predicted by the researchers, the negative implications of social distancing behaviours are prevalent regardless of social support or social and social network size (Marroquín et al., 2020).

The Effects of the Pandemic on College Students in China

The Chinese government, medical and healthcare providers, and the general public have suffered tremendously from the pressure of COVID-19 (Cao, et al., 2020). At the time of this study, the now global pandemic had just begun in China and was considered an epidemic. The spread of the virus and its associated intervention, such as social distancing, measures in schools and universities specifically was expected to have implications on the mental health of students (Cao, et al., 2020). Previous research and reports have discussed the psychological implications of COVID-19 on the general public, patients, medical staff, children, and older adults (Cao, et al., 2020). However, this was the first study to bring light to the mental health of students attending college and its associations with the epidemic (Cao, et al., 2020).

In this investigation, a sample of college students from Changzhi medical college completed a questionnaire for information, which included the 7-item Generalized Anxiety Disorder Scale (GAD-7) (Cao, et al., 2020). The GAD-7 is a reliable and efficient instrument used for screening and detecting anxiety disorders, hence its continuous use in research and clinical practice (Cao, et al., 2020). In addition, health emergencies have been shown to be accompanied by psychological implications such as anxiety, fear, and worry (Cao, et al., 2020). The purpose of this research was to investigate psychological effects on college students, as well as its influencing factors, during the COVID-19 epidemic (Cao, et al., 2020). The questionnaires answered by the college students indicated that 24.9% of them had experienced anxiety due to COVID-19, with 0.9% being severe (Cao, et al., 2020). However, the researchers speculated that the reported anxiety levels may have been due to the social distancing and the separation of individuals during quarantine (Cao, et al., 2020). The reason for this postulation is the fact that anxiety disorders and their associated symptoms are more common when there is a lack of interpersonal communication (Cao, et al., 2020).

Conclusion

It is anticipated that the COVID-19 pandemic will have adverse implications on mental health, which needs to be addressed with research, policy, and clinical science (Marroquín et al., 2020). Especially during the start of the pandemic, large-scale interventions such as physical distancing and quarantine are crucial in decreasing the rate of transmission and mortality (Tull et al., 2020). The necessity is due to the lack of effective infection prevention efforts, wide-spread testing and tracking, and pharmacological interventions for COVID-19 (Tull et al., 2020). The studies mentioned provide confirmation that stay-at-home orders, as well as social distancing measures are associated with negative psychological consequences (Marroquín et al., 2020). On a positive note, findings from a study convey that the COVID-19 pandemic has increased the number of individuals that seek social support, as they are attempting to adjust to the drastic change in lifestyle (Tull et al., 2020).

Despite its negative implications, social distancing measures are crucial in controlling the SARS-CoV-2 virus, and should not be eradicated (Marroquín et al., 2020). Instead, the focus should be on the implementation of mental health interventions as well as methods to increase social relationships and social support to diminish the negative effects (Marroquín et al., 2020). Particularly, the importance of tele-mental health services will become prevalent, as the pandemic continues to progress (Tull et al., 2020). These services need to become more readily accessible for individuals in quarantine that practice physical distancing (Tull et al., 2020). In addition, the current effective mental health interventions could be improved by focusing on the impact of the social disruption in psychological responses throughout the COVID-19 pandemic, as well as, telehealth services aiding the individuals most impacted during these unprecedented times (Tull et al., 2020).

However, it is important to consider that the studies mentioned were conducted towards the beginning of the pandemic, in 2020. As of 2021, multiple vaccines are readily available, with about 5 billion shots administered globally. The aforementioned COVID-19 restrictions, including social distancing and lock-down, have been diminished. The SARS-CoV-2 virus has yet to be eradicated, nonetheless, the future looks promising as the world slowly works its way towards returning to normal.

Chapter 2:

COVID-19
and the
Central Nervous System

Ann Ping

Introduction

In December 2019, a novel viral outbreak was reported in Wuhan, Hubei Province, China. This disease, coronavirus disease 2019 (COVID-19), is caused by severe acute respiratory syndrome coronavirus 2 (SARS-CoV-2). Patients with COVID-19 develop an acute lower tract respiratory infection, which could include difficulty breathing, a dry cough, and fever (Vargas et al., 2020). Aside from respiratory symptoms, there is also evidence that SARS-CoV-2 infection is associated with neurological manifestations, such as headache, delirium, anosmia (loss of smell), and ageusia (loss of taste) (Vargas et al., 2020). In fact, in a study with 214 patients, 36.4% presented with neurological symptoms (Mao et al., 2020). Moreover, COVID-19 patients with central nervous system (CNS) symptoms exhibited lower lymphocyte (a type of white blood cell) counts compared with patients without CNS symptoms (Mao et al., 2020). Because low lymphocyte counts are indicative of immunosuppression, it is likely that severe SARS-CoV-2 infection is associated with neurological alterations (Mao et al., 2020).

Glial cells are non-neuronal cells in the CNS and peripheral nervous system (PNS) and their general role is the protection and support of neurons. Glial cells in the CNS, such as microglia and astrocytes, play important roles in the brain response to neuroinflammation and neurodegenerative diseases (Vargas et al., 2020). Glial cell dysfunction has been observed in many cases of neuroinflammatory diseases (Vargas et al., 2020). Given this information, it is hypothesized that SARS-CoV-2 infection may cause CNS inflammation, subsequently resulting in neurological symptoms (Vargas et al., 2020). This chapter will review the research on the effect of COVID-19 on the CNS and the resulting neurological manifestations. Specifically, this chapter will first review the hypotheses that explain SARS-CoV-2 neuroinvasion, then discuss anosmia as a neurological manifestation and its effect on mental health, and then finally address the association between delirium and glial cell dysfunction.

Hypotheses Explaining
SARS-CoV-2 Neuroinvasion

Currently, there are two proposed pathways that allow SARS-CoV-2 to access the CNS: the first is via hematogenous access (through the blood) and the second is via retrograde (backwards-directed) neuronal routes (Vargas et al., 2020).

Hematogenous access can occur in several ways. The virus could infect endothelial cells from the blood-brain barrier (a highly selective permeable border of endothelial cells in the vasculature of the CNS) or it could infect the epithelial cells of the blood-cerebrospinal fluid barrier (a membrane composed of epithelial cells that separates blood from cerebrospinal fluid) (Vargas et al., 2020). The blood-brain barrier and the blood-cerebrospinal fluid barrier prevent the passage of most blood-borne substances into the brain while allowing the passage of vital nutrients, wastes, and other necessary substances. It plays an important role in keeping viruses out of the brain. The virus could also infect leukocytes (white blood cells) which then subsequently enter the CNS (Vargas et al., 2020).

In contrast, access through retrograde neuronal routes involves first entering the olfactory nerve located in the upper part of the nasal cavity, then the olfactory bulb, to enter the brain (Li et al., 2020). The olfactory nerve belongs to the PNS and terminates in the olfactory bulb in the CNS (Alam et al., 2020). The travel of SARS-CoV-2 through nerves from the PNS to the CNS constitutes retrograde neuronal passage. Studies have found high expression of angiotensin converting enzyme 2 (ACE2), the main coronavirus receptor, in the olfactory bulb and endothelial cells, supporting the hypotheses that SARS-CoV-2 enters the CNS via retrograde neuronal routes and/or via the blood-brain barrier, respectively (Vargas et al., 2020).

Anosmia as a Neurological Manifestation

The loss or reduction of smell and taste is recognized as one of the primary symptoms of COVID-19 (Butowt & von Bartheld, 2020). In fact, 44.1% of COVID-19 patients report olfactory deficits, 43.3% of COVID-19 patients report taste deficits, and the prevalence of any chemosensory deficits is 49.0% (Butowt & von Bartheld, 2020). Anosmia and ageusia are typically transient and last from a few days to about 2 weeks, but can persist after the period of infection (Butowt & von Bartheld, 2020). It is interesting that anosmia is an early symptom of COVID-19 because it lends support to the hypothesis that SARS-CoV-2 may take an olfactory, neuron-to-neuron route to the brain (Vargas et al., 2020; Butowt & von Bartheld, 2020). However, the mechanism of anosmia in COVID-19 is still debated. Some neurologists argue against the retrograde neuronal route hypothesis, pointing out that ACE2, although expressed in the olfactory bulb, is not expressed in olfactory receptor neurons located in the nasal epithelium (Butowt & von Bartheld, 2020). However, there is evidence that some stem cells in the olfactory epithelium express low levels of ACE2; using this information, other neurologists suggest that it is entirely possible that SARS-CoV-2 may enter the stem cells (Butowt & von Bartheld, 2020). Subsequently, when the stem cells turn into mature olfactory receptor neurons, the virus may be transferred into the olfactory bulb and spread through the rest of the CNS (Butowt & von Bartheld, 2020).

Anosmia, Aguesia, and Mental Health

Anosmia and ageusia are associated with poor mental health. For instance, individuals with olfactory dysfunction often have symptoms of depression (Kohli et al., 2016). In fact, the prevalence of depression in patients with olfactory dysfunction ranges from 40% to 76% (Kohli et al., 2016). This is a staggeringly high prevalence, indicating that anosmia is likely a significant contributor to poor mental health among even mild cases of COVID-19. Explanations for the association between anosmia and the development of secondary depression focus on the essential nature of olfaction in daily life (Kohli et al., 2016). Olfaction helps people to detect fires, gas leaks, or poisonous fumes; patients with reduced olfaction may experience anxiety over their dulled awareness towards daily hazards (Kohli et al., 2016). Additionally, olfaction plays a large role in food experience. It allows individuals to enjoy meals and cooking as well as detect spoiled and inedible food (Kohli et al., 2016). A loss of enjoyment of food may subsequently result in self-isolation as one becomes less inclined to socialize over meals (Kohli et al., 2016).

At a neurological level, the olfactory bulb has strong neural connections with the limbic system, the part of the brain which is responsible for emotional processing (Kohli et al., 2016). In fact, many of the emotional and behavioural responses processed in the limbic system are related to survival (Kohli et al., 2016). In the past, human survival was largely dependent on the sense of smell because predators, prey, and edible foods could be recognized through smell (Kohli et al., 2016). As the neocortex (the part of the brain responsible for higher cognitive functioning) developed, the brain became less reliant on the neural connections between the olfactory bulb and the limbic organs (Kohli et al., 2016). However, olfactory projections to core limbic structures, such as the hippocampus and amygdala remain (Kohli et al., 2016).

The neural connections between the limbic system and the olfactory bulb may explain the link between olfaction and mental health at a neurological level. In a study where the olfactory bulbs were removed from rat brains, the dysfunction of various cellular processes within the hippocampus consistent with a depressed state was reported (Morales-Medina et al., 2017). Neurologists also suggest that dulled olfaction may decrease the intensity of stimulus from the olfactory bulb to the limbic system, limiting the effective management of emotion, ultimately resulting in enhanced feelings of sadness, fear, or loneliness (Kohli et al., 2016).

It is also interesting and important to note that a bidirectional relationship exists between olfaction and depression (Kohli et al., 2016). Depressed individuals have diminished olfactory functioning when compared with non-depressed controls (Kohli et al., 2016).

Among individuals who suffer from COVID-19-specific anosmia and ageusia, the research shows a similar pattern: the depression risk for these patients is heightened by 30% (Yom-Tov et al., 2021). The risk of developing depressive symptoms is considerable amongst patients of COVID-19 who experience anosmia and/or ageusia. When taken into account along with other causes of COVID-19 related mental health effects, it becomes clear that further attention should be paid to the psychological needs of COVID-19 patients.

Delirium and Glial Cells

Among the neurological manifestations reported amongst COVID-19 patients, delirium is the most common, occuring in almost 30% of patients (Vargas et al., 2020). Delirium is characterized by acute disturbances in cognition, attention, memory, the sleep-wake cycle, and perception (Sfera et al., 2015). In the context of infectious diseases, delirium can be caused by direct viral CNS infection and neuroinflammation (Vargas et al., 2020). The excessive production of inflammatory mediators (cytokines that promote an inflammatory response) may cause the blood-brain barrier to break down and/ or astrocytes and microglia to activate (Vargas et al., 2020). This subsequently results in a neurotransmitter imbalance which can cause delirium (Vargas et al., 2020). These neurotransmitters include dopamine, γ-aminobutyric acid (GABA), and acetylcholine (Tsuruta & Oda, 2016). Among the many proposed pathophysiologies of delirium, one of the more promising ones in the context of COVID-19 is that glial cells in the CNS produce a neurotoxic response which translates into neuronal damage and manifests as delirium (Vargas et al., 2020). However, if the role of glial cells is to protect neurons, why is it that they would damage neurons during viral infection? It is suggested that astrocytes and microglia have a duality in their phenotype. In other words, this means that these glial cells have either neurotoxic or neuroprotective properties depending on age, infectious stimuli, and physiological condition (Vargas et al., 2020).

Some studies with other viruses show that microglial cells sometimes demonstrate an antagonistic response, in contrast to their neuroprotective role of restricting viral replication and maintaining CNS homeostasis (Vargas et al., 2020). This occurs when microglial cells are overactivated during viral or bacterial infection (Vargas et al., 2020). These overactivated microglia can either directly induce neuronal damage, or activate astrocytes or T lymphocytes which subsequently induce cell death (Vargas et al., 2020).

In combination with clinical evidence from COVID-19 patients, the conclusions made regarding microglial response to other viral infections suggest that not only are glial cells targets of SARS-CoV-2 to promote viral dissemination in the CNS, but also that microglial cells could promote a neurotoxic response, causing neuronal death and delirium as a clinical manifestation (Vargas et al., 2020).

Astrocytes are similar to microglial cells in that they also exhibit neurotoxic or neuroprotective properties depending on the circumstance (Vargas et al., 2020). The cytokines that astrocytes produce in response to infection may be anti-inflammatory or pro-inflammatory (Vargas et al., 2020). Anti-inflammatory cytokines help reduce brain inflammation, but pro-inflammatory cytokines do the opposite (Vargas et al., 2020). A study involving mouse hepatitis virus (MHV) showed that highly neurovirulent MHV strains induced the release of pro-inflammatory cytokines (Li et al., 2004). Overall, microglial cells and astrocytes possess the interesting ability to reduce or exacerbate inflammation depending on the severity of the viral infection. Moreover, evidence shows that glial cells in the brains of older people are more likely to produce neurotoxic response; this is consistent with the finding that older COVID-19 patients are more likely to experience delirium as a symptom (Vargas et al., 2020).

Conclusion

This chapter focused on the effect of SARS-CoV-2 infection on the CNS, covering the hypotheses addressing SARS-CoV-2 neuroinvasion, how anosmia can be explained as a neurological manifestation, the effects of anosmia and ageusia on patient mental health, and the role of glial cells in delirium. Ultimately, although COVID-19 is primarily regarded as a respiratory illness, an increasing amount of studies have suggested or confirmed effects in other organs, such as the brain. This places greater emphasis on the psychological needs of COVID-19 patients, suggesting that more measures may need to be put in place that treat patient mental health. Finally, this chapter may also serve as a word of caution to individuals who take COVID-19 infection lightly—even mild cases can present with olfactory dysfunction, which increases the risk of poor mental health, and even depression.

Chapter 3:

COVID-19, Mental Health, and the Rise of a Shadow Pandemic

Vedanshi Vala

Content Warning:
This chapter discusses abuse, violence, and suicide. Please seek the support of local agencies, such as crisis support lines or mental health professionals, if required.

Introduction

In solidarity, we must stand next to survivors and victims of domestic abuse, as allies in their journey of healing, their battle against trauma, and their fight for basic human rights. It is, however, not just their fight. We must, as a human society, together advocate for a safer world for all. This chapter will explore the interconnection between domestic abuse and mental health impacts on survivors, as well as mental health intervention as a means of both reducing abuse and being crucial to the healing process of survivors. Specifically, these issues will be investigated contextually with implications of the COVID-19 pandemic in consideration. The first section of this chapter discusses the prevalence and mental health effects of domestic abuse on survivors. Though both men and women report experiencing abuse, the scope of this chapter is restricted to the experiences of women who have survived domestic abuse. While there is never, under no circumstances, a valid excuse for domestic abuse, this chapter will explore its underlying causes in the context of mental health decline during the COVID-19 pandemic. The objective is to understand that countermeasures can be taken by mental health professionals to detect and, through appropriate intervention, reduce the likelihood of an individual perpetrating domestic violence. Moreover, this chapter aims to foster greater empathy and support for survivors of such trauma through informing allies with insight from the literature.

The Prevalence and Effects of Domestic Abuse on Survivors

Had it not been for the battered women's movement in the 1970s, domestic abuse against women may never have been classified as a crime (Martin, 1997, as cited in Wilson, 2005). Human society has come a long way in recognizing women's rights in the past few decades alone, yet the rampancy of violence and abuse warrants greater efforts to counteract this issue. Studies in Australia found that, depending on the definition of abuse employed by the survey, survivors of partner abuse ranged between 2.1 to 28 percent of the respondents (Hegarty and Roberts, 1998). Grasping the prevalence of domestic abuse requires an understanding of the manner in which such data is obtained, and the potential inaccuracies inherent in such a system (Hegarty and Roberts, 1998). For instance, to know how many actual cases of domestic abuse occur, they would need to be reported—and domestic abuse has been on the rise, according to many women's shelters (Martin, 1997, as cited in Wilson, 2005). Advocates may be disheartened by the increasing number of reported cases each year; however, this does not necessarily mean that abuse itself has increased (Martin, 1997, as cited in Wilson, 2005). Rather, these numbers can be indicative of improvements in awareness on what constitutes abuse, as well as in the greater willingness of survivors to report their abusers (Martin, 1997, as cited in Wilson, 2005). Because social context is of a constantly evolving nature, trends in domestic abuse prevalence should be studied in parallel to other such factors which can affect how many cases of abuse are reported out of the number of actual cases occurring. This may mean that academia can never fully understand whether domestic abuse is increasing or decreasing. That being said, it remains that there are far too many reports of domestic abuse, and action is required given its immediate and long-term effects.

As with other traumatic events, domestic abuse can have long-lasting effects on the health and well-being of survivors. Domestic abuse "does not occur in a vacuum" as its effects "on women and children touch every aspect of their lives and the lives of those around them" (Wilson, 2005, p. 2). Abuse comes in many forms, and psychological abuse may be even more detrimental to the survivor than physical abuse is, with 72% of respondents in a study reporting emotional abuse to have affected them more severely than physical abuse (Sackett and Saunders, 1999). In a study investigating the impact of psychological abuse on women, the researchers categorized such abuse into four distinct behaviours, being: ridiculing, criticizing, ignoring, and controlling (Sackett and Saunders, 1999). The study found that women who seek support from shelters had experienced far more ridicule and control from their abuser in comparison to women not in shelters (Sackett and Saunders, 1999). Being ridiculed by abusers is strongly correlated to low self-esteem in survivors, while all forms of psychological and physical abuse may lead to both low self-esteem and depression (Sackett and Saunders, 1999). A different study similarly examines the mental health consequences for survivors of intimate partner abuse, which they categorize into physical violence, sexual coercion, emotional abuse, and stalking (Mechanic et al., 2008). The authors report that, independent of effects of injuries sustained from physical or sexual violence, psychological abuse and stalking both contribute towards a greater likelihood of posttraumatic stress disorder (PTSD) and depression (Mechanic et al., 2008). These findings are corroborated by yet another study, which finds that the women subjected to sexual violence or coerced to participate in sexual acts experience more symptoms of PTSD, as well as an increased likelihood of developping PTSD (Norwood and Murphy, 2012).

The prevalence of domestic abuse is alarming, and its effects are extremely damaging to the well-being of the survivor, and those closest to them. The next section examines the COVID-19 pandemic as a factor which is conducive to environments of heightened opportunity for aggressors to harm their victims, bringing greater attention to the shadow pandemic which has ensued.

COVID-19 and the Shadow Pandemic

As discussed in the previous section, domestic abuse has many long-term effects on the mental health of survivors. During the COVID-19 pandemic, increases in domestic abuse due to isolation, economic pressures, and fear have been attributed to observations of heightening risk of psychiatric disorders leading to suicidality (Banerjee et al.,

2021). The HIV/AIDS pandemic in China, whose implications on women were studied by a paper years prior to the COVID-19 pandemic, states that economic pressures from unemployment are linked to increases in domestic violence (Renwick, 2002). A similar narrative is likely applicable to the COVID-19 pandemic, where financial strain from skyrocketing unemployment may contribute to aggression in homes. This demonstrates how domestic abuse, mental health, and economic disparities may all contribute to the same cyclical, societal problem. This potentially highlights an interconnection between the health crisis of the COVID-19 pandemic and exacerbated shadow pandemics of poor mental health and heightened domestic abuse.

Is there a correlation between unmanaged mental illness and likelihood of perpetrating domestic abuse? There have been findings suggesting that perpetrators of abuse comprise a portion of patients seeking mental health services, highlighting an opportunity for mental health services to potentially reduce domestic violence through the appropriate response (Bhavsar et al., 2021). This finding can be used to identify and ratify underlying causes of abusive behaviour, such as unmanaged substance abuse disorders, unhealthy familial examples, and childhood adversity (Bhavsar et al., 2021). Moreover, mental health professionals identifying abusive behaviour in an individual can aid them in protecting partners and family members of the patient, potentially increasing their personal safety by preemptive intervention against domestic violence (Bhavsar et al., 2021). On a note of clarity, these findings are not meant to equate mental illness to domestic abuse perpetration, but rather, how mental health services can identify such behaviour and prevent its escalation. A study investigated the use of mental health services in the detection of abuse perpetration, and found that individuals using mental health services considered it acceptable to be asked about domestic violence while accessing a mental health service, but some mental health professionals were against such routine inquiry (Trevillion et al., 2012). One of the reasons expressed by professionals for such discomfort was related to a lack of clarity on reporting obligations upon discovery of a domestic violence case (Trevillion et al., 2012). Ensuring that mental health professionals can identify abusive behaviours and provide the required intervention has the potential to reduce mental health-related causation of domestic violence (Bhavsar et al., 2021). During the COVID-19 pandemic, which saw a slew of lockdowns globally, domestic abuse increase is paralleled with a decrease in its visibility due to social isolation (Bhavsar et al., 2021). For instance, if an individual was being subjected to physical violence at home, their injuries are less likely to be noticed by coworkers because they no longer work in-person, due to lockdowns, where such observations can be made. It is in such a situation, where there is heightened opportunity for abuse to occur in isolated domestic environments, that access to mental health programs is crucial to the prevention of abuse (Bhavsar et al., 2021).

Mental health services certainly play an important role in identifying those who are likely to perpetrate abuse; however, they are especially crucial for victims and survivors. During the COVID-19 pandemic, women facing abusive domestic environments have experienced many new challenges. In an interview, Vanessa Waechtler, a counsellor at CHIMO Community Services, asserted that "women are trapped, more so, with their abusers, 'cause they're spending more time in the home [and] their abuser's spending more time in the home" meaning there is greater opportunity for the occurrence of violence (BOLT Safety Society, 2021). Waechtler continued to explain how due to the economic toll of the pandemic, many women and their abusive partners are out of work, and opportunities to leave the house as well as connect with supportive networks of colleagues and friends become limited (BOLT Safety Society, 2021). Yet another challenge posed by the pandemic is barriers created to accessing mental health support services. Waechtler shared how it sometimes became difficult for clients to attend their sessions, because "they would have to make up an excuse as to where they were going", and even how lockdowns meant phone therapy sessions had to happen with the client's abuser in a nearby room (BOLT Safety Society, 2021). "A fair number of my clients had to drop out of counselling back in March because they just couldn't get the privacy in their own home to do a phone session with me", Waechtler stated grimly (BOLT Safety Society, 2021). Moreover, Waechtler explained how the COVID-19 pandemic has introduced new forms of abuse in co-parenting situations, such as arguments regarding their child or children selecting a social bubble during lockdown, and disputes about the child's safety during the pandemic (BOLT Safety Society, 2021). "I don't think that you're social-distancing properly, you don't care about our kid's safety!" said Waechtler, providing an example of what such an argument could consist of (BOLT Safety Society, 2021).

There are many complex, connected issues pertaining to mental health, domestic abuse, and economic disparities which have been aggravated by the COVID-19 pandemic. It is a solemnizing reality; however, through efforts to resolve these underlying, systemic issues, as well as increased empathy and allyship, there can be hope for safer homes for all.

A Beacon of Hope: Empathy and Allyship

Survivors and victims are not alone in their journey. They should not be, at the very least, for society at all levels should unify to fight against this crisis of human rights. The solution to safer communities starts with systemic reform to foster a culture of consent. Empathy and allyship for survivors are both key elements in such a pursuit. Until the end of the COVID-19 pandemic, until such a time that the economic issues are resolved, until there is adequate and timely access to mental health care services, women will unfortunately continue to be vulnerable to abuse. Waechtler said in her interview that "a lot of women know that this is gonna be a long haul" (BOLT Safety Society, 2021). As allies, individuals can play a role of great significance in a victim or survivor's journey by being a source of strength, comfort, and support. This starts by refusing to blame the survivor and by holding the abuser accountable. No matter the economic burden, no matter the mental health challenges, abuse cannot ever be validated or excused, but it can be prevented with appropriate mental health intervention and lessening of economic disparities. Societal reform for a survivor-centric narrative necessitates providing survivors of sexual assault and domestic abuse with the resources they need to rebuild their lives after encountering such traumatic situations. Waechtler shared that the resources required to provide such programming have been made available during the pandemic, and "it's great that this is not being forgotten in the madness of our world right now [because] abuse still exists, and it's intensifying" (BOLT Safety Society, 2021). In the midst of chaos, and reaching deep within a harrowing reality, the ongoing and imperative work at all levels of the community to support survivors and prevent abuse scintillates as a beacon of hope.

Conclusion

This chapter sought to explore the concerning and exacerbated prevalence of domestic abuse reports during the COVID-19 pandemic, and to understand it within the context of underlying issues related to mental health. It was established in the first section that domestic abuse has lasting effects on the lives of women who have survived abusive relationships, their children, and their loved ones. To reiterate, though statistics on domestic abuse may be showing an increase in numbers each year, this does not necessarily mean abuse has increased; rather, it can be indicative of more women being both willing and able to report their abuser. This may demonstrate progress in advocacy efforts, such as those made to flip the victim-blaming narrative and put the onus on the perpetrator of violence. However, it remains that domestic violence against women is an imminent threat to the wellbeing and safety of the entirety of human society, given that its effects transcend the immediately-affected victims and survivors. Moreover, the second section explored the correlation between mental health decline during the COVID-19 and other pandemics with the exacerbation of shadow crises, such as that of domestic abuse. Ratifying underlying economic disparities, increasing awareness about this issue, and promoting greater access to resources for mental well-being may aid in reducing the number of cases of violence against women. Though a problem of alarming magnitude, there are ways that individuals can strive to be better allies for survivors, as discussed in the third section of this chapter. All in all, there are ways forward towards safer communities. Taking steps towards that needed change must continue to happen in unity. Ultimately, the issue of women's safety is one that concerns all people.

Chapter 4:

How the COVID-19 Pandemic has Affected Student and Healthcare Worker Mental Health and Well-being

Omar Abdul Hadi

Introduction

Mental health is one of the leading barriers that prevents academic success (Son et al., 2020). Mental health issues can lead to lack of motivation, confidence, and concentration which are all vital factors that determine one's success (Son et al., 2020). Generally, university students are considered a vulnerable population, suffering from higher levels of depression, anxiety and substance abuse than the general population (Browning et al., 2021).

There is no doubt that the COVID-19 pandemic has caused mental health issues for individuals of all ages. The pandemic has influenced practically every sector such as healthcare, tourism, agriculture, finance and many more (Lee et al., 2021). More and more people have been forced to stay home in self isolation to prevent the spread of the virus at a societal level; this isolation has put people at an increased risk of mental health issues (Lee et al., 2021). University and college students have been forced to give up the 'college experience' due to campus closures and the shift to online learning (Lee et al., 2021). Deprivation from social gatherings, parties, study groups and social interactions has triggered a decline in mental health amongst the general student population (Lee et al., 2021).

How the Pandemic has Affected The Mental Health of Workers

While students have been affected greatly by this pandemic, groups across all professions have also suffered a mental toll. Health care workers have been carrying a great responsibility on the frontlines and, as a result, have suffered immensely. Health care workers are at higher risk of adverse mental health outcomes due to the nature of their work, and this risk increases during times of infectious disease outbreak (Spoorthy et al., 2020). For example, one year after the SARS outbreak in 2003, health care workers were six times more likely to experience psychiatric symptoms as compared to the general population (Spoorthy et al., 2020). One to two years after the SARS outbreak, more than one third of healthcare workers that were in contact with SARS patients still reported emotional exhaustion (Spoorthy et al., 2020). It is estimated that 34 to 37% of healthcare workers working with COVID patients suffer from insomnia (difficulty falling asleep), 29% report feeling burnt out, 20 to 51% suffer from depression symptoms, 12 to 45% suffer from constant anxiety symptoms, 19 to 51% suffer from post traumatic stress disorder (PTSD), 31% suffer from acute stress syndrome and 34% have a combination of mental health issues (Spoorthy et al., 2020). The reasons for such adverse psychological outcomes in healthcare workers range from excessive workload and work hours, inadequate personal protective equipment, over-enthusiastic media news, and feeling inadequately supported. Another important reason for psychological impact is the infection rate among medical staff and peers. The sudden reversal of roles from being a frontline worker to a patient might lead to helplessness, stigma, fear, frustration and fear of discrimination among the medical staff (Spoorthy et al., 2020). A cross sectional survey conducted by the branch of psychiatry in the Chinese nursing association was used to assess whether nurses working in emergency departments were mentally and emotionally exhausted (An et al., 2020). Emergency room nurses are responsible for a wide variety of tasks, including life-threatening clinical situations that require immediate attention (An et al., 2020). Depression was measured using the Patient-Health questionnaire (PHQ) (Chinese version) (An et al., 2020). The PHQ is a tool widely used in clinical settings. Each question is scored from 0-3 and a total score of five or more indicates depression (An et al., 2020). A total score between five and nine indicates mild depression, a score between ten and fourteen indicates moderate depression, a score between fifteen and nineteen indicates moderate-to-severe depression and a score greater than twenty indicates severe depression (An et al., 2020). Approximately half of the nurses surveyed showed signs of depression (An et al., 2020). Another study conducted at a hospital in

Wuhan, China, from February 9 to March 15, 2020 aimed to identify, by interviewing 23 individuals, the process of psychological change of nurses during the COVID-19 outbreak (Sampaio et al., 2021). The findings showed that nurses' psychological changes occurred in three stages: the first stage is referred to as the early stage (Sampaio et al., 2021). The early stage is when their psychological experience is mainly ambivalent (Sampaio et al., 2021). The second stage is referred to as the middle stage and it is where one's psychological characteristics are identified as anxiety, depression, fear and irritation (Sampaio et al., 2021). Finally, the last stage is referred to as the later stage. During this stage, nurses' psychological adaptation began to occur (Sampaio et al., 2021).

Studies on How The Pandemic Has Affected Student Mental Health

A study on how the COVID-19 pandemic has affected student mental health was conducted at an unnamed university in Texas, United States in 2020 (Son et al., 2020). A total of 195 students were interviewed via Zoom during the lockdown in April 2020 (Son et al., 2020). Participants were asked questions related to how they were affected in different areas such as lifestyle, academics and mental health (Son et al., 2020). Out of the 195 participants, 31 (16%) reported severe concerns about their general health, 86 (44%) reported moderate health concerns, 60 (31%) reported mild health concerns and 18 (9%) reported no health concerns (Son et al., 2020). When participants were asked about disruptions in sleeping patterns, 38% of individuals reported severe disruptions to sleeping patterns, 27% reported moderate changes in sleep, 21% reported mild changes in sleep and 14% reported no changes in sleeping patterns (Son et al., 2020). Therefore, a total of 86% of participants reported disruptions in sleeping patterns (Son et al., 2020). Over 86% of participants reported increased self isolation due to the COVID-19 pandemic with over 54% of individuals stating that the pandemic has significantly decreased their interactions with other people (Son et al., 2020). A large majority of individuals surveyed (89%) stated that the COVID-19 pandemic has caused them to be anxious about their academic performance and their future academic plans (Son et al., 2020). Participants reported that the biggest challenge was the transition to online classes (Son et al., 2020). Furthermore, all students were concerned with sudden changes in class syllabi, difficulty transitioning to online classes, quality of online learning and technical difficulties with online learning applications (Son et al., 2020). Out of the 195 individuals that participated in this survey, 8% of participants reported that they had serious suicidal thoughts (Son et al., 2020). These suicidal thoughts were a result of depression, problems with academic performance, family problems, as well as insecurities and fear (Son et al., 2020). 46% of participants reported having depression and depressive thoughts attributed to loneliness, insecurity, powerlessness or hopelessness, overthinking and fear of poor academic performance (Son et al., 2020).

A second study conducted in 2020 showed similar results (Lee et al., 2021). Two hundred domestic U.S students aged 18-24 completed a survey consisting of 14 multiple choice questions (Lee et al., 2021). The first question asked participants how the COVID-19 pandemic has affected their overall mental health (Lee et al., 2021). 83.6% of participants reported an increase in anxiety, depression and loneliness while only 10.6% of participants reported that they were unaffected and had no increase in those three symptoms (Lee et al., 2021). Participants were then asked what specifically was causing their increase in mental health problems (Lee et al., 2021). 19.2% of participants reported that they were most concerned with their school and continuing education, 19.0% were worried about their proactivity, 15.9% were worried about finances, 10.8% were worried about future opportunities and job offers, 5% feared contracting and being sick of the virus and only 6.8% reported that they were at ease (Lee et al., 2021). The following question asked students if it was easier or harder to complete a semester online as compared to in-person. 61% of responses stated that it was more difficult to complete a semester online, 32.7% of students reported that an online semester was easier than a regular semester and 6.4% reported no change in difficulty (Lee et al., 2021). The next question on the survey asked participants how the COVID-19 pandemic has affected their physical health (Lee et al., 2021). Half of the participants reported that they gained weight due to increased eating and other bad habits, 20.2% reported that they lost weight and felt or looked better than before the pandemic began and 16.6% reported no change in physical health (Lee et al., 2021). Next, the survey asked students to state what they spent most of their time doing during the pandemic. Almost 71% of students reported that they spend most of their time watching shows or television (Lee et al., 2021). This is especially concerning as an excess of screen time can have a detrimental effect on general health and mental health (Lee et al., 2021). This is because more screen time can lead to lower levels of physical activity which puts one at an increased risk of obesity and other diseases which may ultimately affect one's mental health. Apart from watching shows and television, 30.5% of participants reported reading books in their free time, 39.6% spent most of their time exercising and playing sports, 34.9% reported learning new skills and hobbies, 33.6% were cooking and baking, 29.5% spent their time working and volunteering and 8% said they did not do anything productive during the pandemic (Lee et al., 2021). Participants were also asked if the pandemic has affected their relationship with friends and family. 27.8% of students reported an improvement in their relationship with friends and family, 45.7% reported a decrease in their relationships and 26.5% reported no change in their relationships (Lee et al., 2021). Finally, participants were asked how the pandemic has affected their current and future plans (Lee et al., 2021). 26.4% of participants reported that the pandemic has not affected any current or future plans, 27.1% lost an internship or job offer, 22.9% of participants were taking a gap year from school, and only 16.6% of participants responded that the pandemic opened beneficial opportunities for them (Lee et al., 2021).

A third study was conducted to see the effects of the COVID-19 pandemic on medical students in Changzi, Shanxi, China (Cao et al., 2020). The target population was 7143 undergraduate students from Changzi medical college (Cao et al., 2020). After all the participants completed an assigned questionnaire, researchers analyzed the results to determine anxiety levels with the population (Cao et al., 2020). 5367 respondents (75.4% of respondents) reported that they had normal anxiety levels due to the pandemic, 1518 or 21.3% of respondents reported mild levels of anxiety, 196 or 2.7% of respondents reported moderate levels of anxiety and 62 or 0.9% of respondents reported severe levels of anxiety due to the pandemic (Cao et al., 2020). Causes of increased anxiety included the surge in COVID-19 cases and its risk on the general population, switching to online learning and shortage of masks and personal protective equipment (PPE)
(Cao et al., 2020).

Conclusion

Many individuals worldwide have been affected by the COVID-19 pandemic. Health care workers fighting against COVID-19 have experienced many psychological difficulties. Excessive workload and work hours, inadequate personal protective equipment, over-enthusiastic media news, and feeling inadequately supported are all reasons that frontline workers suffer from psychological stress. Frontline workers of all professions including doctors and nurses have been clinically diagnosed with depression, anxiety and many other mental health disorders. The drastic changes in the work environment that COVID-19 has changed for these healthcare workers has caused immense stress and challenges that have hindered their mental health. Depression rates among emergency department nurses increased significantly as a result of the very stressful nature of their work, especially during the pandemic. Emergency department nurses are on the frontline on a regular basis, dealing with life or death situations on a regular basis which can really take a toll on one's mental health. Students have also been greatly affected by this pandemic. Many studies have been conducted to study the effects of the pandemic on mental health. From these studies it can be concluded that the pandemic has affected students differently. It is evident from the studies conducted above that during the pandemic, self isolation has greatly increased; the majority of students experience increased anxiety due to academic performance and a significant number of relationships were harmed due to self isolation measures. The majority of students (approximately 71%) of students spent most of their time watching shows or television which has had a higher toll on their mental health.

Chapter 5:

The Impact of COVID-19 on the Mental Health of Health Care Providers

Joylen Kingsley

Introduction

COVID-19 has changed many aspects of daily life, from human interaction to social and cultural practices. One of the main by-products of drastic life changes has been the significant impact on the public's mental health. There have been countless reminders, promoting the public to seek mental health help if necessary. People have been encouraged to turn to doctors, therapists, nurses, and healthcare workers in general, when they experience COVID-19 related mental distress. But to whom do healthcare professionals turn when they experience depression and anxiety due to the pandemic?

COVID-19 was first discovered in 2019 as a severe respiratory disorder in Wuhan China (Braquehais et al., 2020). Since its discovery, it has spread to more than 200 countries and as of March 2020 has officially been considered a pandemic (Vizheh et al., 2020). As of April 2020, a mere 4 months since the initial outbreak, there have been over 200 000 deaths worldwide (Vizheh et al., 2020). Even countries who have had pandemic plans in place have been overwhelmed by the sheer number of cases and contagiousness of the virus (Braquehais et al., 2020). SARS-CoV-2 has spun the world on its axis, exposing systematic failures in multiple sectors, especially demonstrated by the ill-preparedness of the healthcare system. This lack of preparation has culminated in the sacrifice of both the physical and mental wellbeing of the world's healthcare workers.

Incidences of anxiety, depression, stress and burnout among healthcare professionals have been unprecedented since the start of the pandemic (Eftekhar Ardebili et al., 2021). COVID-19 has caused many health sector workers to fall ill due to infection, and their employment conditions exacerbate fear and stress in the workplace. Workers have had increased concerns due to the death of their colleagues, fear of contracting the illness and their own potential death, pressure from society and their leaders, lack of social support, media pressure and financial burden (Eftekhar Ardebili et al., 2021). This chapter will explore the qualitative and quantitative experience of healthcare workers during the pandemic, to expose the insurmountable sacrifices that they have made for the general public.

Exposure Control for Frontline Healthcare Workers

Pandemic outbreaks have historically caused an increased demand for healthcare workers, but SARS-CoV-2 not only caught workers by surprise, but the speed and efficiency with which it spread heavily outcompeted the pandemic protocols that were already in place (Vizheh et al., 2020). Transmission has been a problem that has particularly caused distress among the general populace (Vizheh et al., 2020). Frontline workers, not limited to healthcare workers, are at particularly high risk, especially with the unpredictable nature of the virus and the subsequent waves in which infectious cases have been rising (Braquehais et al., 2020; di Tella et al., 2020). Studies report high levels of insomnia, emotional symptoms, and burnout, with high prevalence of depressive symptoms and anxiety, ranging from 20-40% and 30-70% respectively (Braquehais et al., 2020). It is difficult to gauge the exact situations of each individual worker as they have each been subjected to their own experiences depending on when or where they were potentially exposed to COVID-19 or when their respective nations implemented COVID-19 protocols (Vizheh et al., 2020). Frontline workers are most likely to contract the virus and have a better understanding of the symptoms as they have seen and cared for patients who have been exposed to SARS-CoV-2. Therefore, it is no surprise that frontline workers who have COVID-19 related clinical responsibilities and workers who have already been infected were more likely to suffer from mental distress (Braquehais et al., 2020). Greater opportunity for exposure has been correlated with greater prevalence of anxiety and depressive symptoms (Braquehais et al., 2020). Distress symptoms and incidence recording via surveys and systematics reviews also depend heavily on the impact of the pandemic. Some surveys were taken when there were an overwhelming number of cases in heavily affected cities, while others were taken in a relatively calm period in less affected areas. (Braquehais et al., 2020). Countries such as Italy were more heavily impacted towards the beginning of the pandemic, while countries such as Brazil have been more heavily affected by the subsequent variants of the original viral strain (Slone et al., 2021). India—who has experienced continuous issues throughout the course of the pandemic, from the initial, almost uncontrollable outbreak to the variants, and lack of vaccines—has reported a 20% increase in mental health cases since the beginning of the pandemic (Kumar & Nayar, 2020). Nurses have been more prone to mental harm than any other provider group, as they form the majority of the healthcare workforce that interacts with patients (Vizheh et al., 2020). They are often in elevated risk and high stress scenarios, therefore corresponding with the idea that increased exposure correlates with increased risk (Braquehais et al., 2020b; Vizheh et al., 2020).

Comparing mental health from SARS to SARS-CoV-2

One study conducted on the mental impact of severe acute respiratory syndrome (SARS) on healthcare workers showed that 77.4% of the study population had signs of anxiety, 74.2% had depressive symptoms, 69.0% had somatic symptoms and 52.3% had insomnia (Vizheh et al., 2020). Surprisingly, SARS-CoV-2 healthcare workers showed lower prevalence of mental health disorders in comparison to SARS healthcare workers potentially due to lowered fatality rates (Vizheh et al., 2020). While lowered mortality rates are a source of comfort, many other sources have caused increased anxiety. Social media and accessibility to news has been a trigger to public fear, especially since not all information presented is factual. During the SARS outbreak, the biggest source of trauma to workers was contact with infectious departments, including the Emergency department and Intensive Care Unit (Vizheh et al., 2020). These findings are also consistent with COVID-19 where one study shows that 70.6% of healthcare workers fear transmission through contact due to their job, especially because of potentially asymptomatic cases (Vizheh et al., 2020). Long term consequences of COVID-19 on mental health can be predicted based on previous pandemics (Ornell et al., 2020). Psychiatric research after the SARS outbreak in 2003 and the Middle East respiratory syndrome (MERS) outbreak in 2015 showed mental distress in 18-57% of providers (Ornell et al., 2020). Serious emotional problems, psychiatric symptoms, and increased stress levels were reported during and after both outbreaks; post-traumatic stress disorder, depression and substance abuse were also predicted after SARS, allowing researchers to make the fair assumption that mental distress will continue for years after the initial outbreak of SARS-CoV-2 (Ornell et al., 2020)

Inhibitors to Proper Care

A qualitative study conducted in Iran exposed the obstacles that further frustrated healthcare workers and emulated conditions faced all around the world throughout the pandemic (Eftekhar Ardebili et al., 2021). Almost 87% of healthcare reported feeling overwhelmed during the initial days of the pandemic: the volume of patients, lack of protective equipment and general ill-preparedness for the situation caused major confusion (Eftekhar Ardebili et al., 2021). The constant changes in protocol and the lack of consistent information manifested itself as fear and anxiety in providers; this was primarily the case during the first months of 2020 (Eftekhar Ardebili et al., 2021). Loss of control over the situation and lessened human interaction were heavily cited causes for initial mental health decline among providers towards the beginning of the pandemic (Eftekhar Ardebili et al., 2021). While initial mental distress was caused by a lack of control, the next major stressor was the inability to act. Anxiety was prevalent in the initial days of the pandemic, but depression dominated afterwards, as mortality rates and hospitalization increased (Eftekhar Ardebili et al., 2021). This was also during the time when exhaustion began to prevail among providers, increasing feelings of frustration (Eftekhar Ardebili et al., 2021). The significance of the Iranian study was the qualitative approach to mental health, as the study results were consistent with other qualitative studies (Eftekhar Ardebili et al., 2021). Prominent levels of fear, stress, helplessness, and hopelessness prevailed both in healthcare workers' personal and career lives, further showing on both an experiential and factual level that mental health among providers is another lesser-known impact of COVID-19.

Professional Burnout

Burnout is experienced in all professions, but exhaustive efforts of healthcare professionals have exacerbated the effects in the last few years. Professional burnout was an issue well before the pandemic: regardless of global conditions, healthcare workers constantly face heavy workloads, strict regulation, and rapid day-to-day changes (Sultana et al., 2020). Pandemic conditions consist of factors that potentiate burnout (Sultana et al., 2020). Significant increase in cases and work hours with limited available resources result in sleep deprivation and more importantly in burnout (Sultana et al., 2020). Burnout is usually diagnosed in long term studies while being related to systemic failures, such as lack of resources and unsavoury climates, but severe triggers such as the COVID-19 pandemic have been known to trigger burnout symptoms Ornell et al., 2020). Physicians are more likely to suffer from depression compared to the national Canadian average, and healthcare professionals that are subject to quarantine and isolation are more likely to experience mental health problems (Sultana et al., 2020). These are the types of incidences that characterize healthcare burnout and the associated negative mental health outcomes (Sultana et al., 2020). The media also plays a role in burnout, where workers are stigmatized and ostracized from the community for their increased exposure to COVID-19 patients. Regardless of the reason for it, healthcare providers are at greater risk of mental harm, due to their position as caretakers of society, and their sacrifice must be acknowledged and taken into account when considering practical solutions for mental health deficits caused by SARS-CoV-19.

Other Concerns in Health Care

Like in the case of burnout, many concerns relating to COVID-19 are systemic in nature. This results in stress not only to the individual worker regarding their personal safety, but regarding the future of their career. Necessary services such as access to comprehensive contraceptives services in the United States and adequate HIV services in China have been halted due to COVID-19 (Comfort et al., 2021; Mi et al., 2021). Providers in frequent and personal contact with patients have also experienced issues such as shared trauma and compassion fatigue because of the intimate nature of their jobs, and because of the connection they manage to build with their patients (Comfort et al., 2021). The most common cause that was cited among health care workers for their depression and anxiety was a feeling of inadequacy regarding the unknown and unpredictable nature of the pandemic (Comfort et al., 2021). In a study conducted in the United States, 58% of reproductive healthcare providers in the study sample had a telehealth option available but were heavily concerned over the uncertainty of when they would be able to see patients again, and with the effectiveness of indirect treatment (Comfort et al., 2021). Outpatient healthcare providers were also concerned about the level of care their non-COVID-19 patients were receiving Comfort et al., 2021).

Conclusion

Interventions must be planned, and accommodation must be made for the heroes who saved and continue to save the countless lives affected by COVID-19. Anxiety and depression in and of itself is concerning but paired with burnout is severely threatening to one's health (Pearman et al., 2020). Similar incidences of distress were seen during SARS and several of those mental health symptoms have been long term, allowing researchers to conclude that the same is possible for COVID-19, where mental health illnesses have the potential to become long term (Pearman et al., 2020).

Organizations such as the World Health Organization have created a 31-point guide for mental health related problems during the pandemic, but it is not unique to the stressors facing healthcare workers (Kumar & Nayar, 2020). It is imperative that mental health professionals are mobilized during this time of need, but that is not possible in many countries. India for example only has 0.29 and 0.07 psychologists available per 100 000 people (Kumar & Nayar, 2020). Doctors have also been sharing tips on improving and maintaining mental health during the pandemic including advice such as: being well rested, eating well and on time, and maintaining contact with colleagues (Alikhani et al., 2020). Physicians also reported that relying on the support of more experienced colleagues and finding time to maintain hobbies was imperative in helping workers assimilate into their COVID-19 provider lifestyle.

This chapter has delved into multiple studies and perspectives regarding the relationship between mental health providers and COVID-19. Despite the differences in sample size and culture, each study concludes that the general mental health of providers has declined since the beginning of the pandemic. Healthcare providers have put their lives at risk for almost two years, their sacrifices must not be taken for granted, and every measure must be placed to maximize their health and wellbeing.

Chapter 6:

The Effects of COVID 19 on Mental Health for the Elderly and the Impoverished

Lilian Yeung

Introduction

With the beginning of social isolation due to the COVID-19 pandemic, many populations of humans were affected, especially with the elderly in terms of their mental health. Typically the elderly living in nursing homes or assisted living facilities are vulnerable to having COVID-19 negatively affect their mental health during this time because of the lack of social support and safety nets that they have in place (Lee et al., 2020). Social support is the group of people that a person relies on to fulfill their social requirements (Lee et al., 2020). The stronger the bonds are, the greater their impact and benefits will be on the person (Lee et al., 2020). As social isolation has forced everyone to rely on technology for communication and social connectedness, this causes a great deal of concern for many. Most elderly are not technologically inclined and prefer in-person contact, which puts them at higher risk of not maintaining their mental health (Rout, 2020). Not only is seniors' mental health affected, but their mental illnesses are also exacerbated with social distancing. Thus, more research and support needs to be made available for the elderly during times of social isolation.

It is not just the elderly that are at a disadvantage during this pandemic, but also the impoverished. Many low income households or poor living facilities have little means of supporting themselves due to their lack of funds and support (Team & Manderson, 2020). Thus, elderly living in poor assisted care facilities may suffer to a greater degree than those living with family or adequate assisted living facilities (Team & Manderson, 2020). Although the governments of many countries have organized methods to provide COVID-19 relief, certain families and people are still struggling due to insufficient COVID-19 support funds and being dismissed from work. As such, many low income peoples' mental health may have been negatively impacted as the stress of the pandemic itself compounds the existing stressors that many people face which includes paying bills on time and sustaining income.

The Effects of COVID 19 on Mental Health for the Elderly

When the social isolation mandate was first put into place, many people bemoaned the fact that they would be alone and endure social isolation. But many of these same people quickly recovered as they explored the various technological ways people stay connected, for instance through social media or the internet. The same cannot be said for the often ignored seniors living in assisted living facilities. The elderly are at a severe disadvantage throughout this social isolation due to a variety of reasons. According to Lee et al. (2020), they are physically more at risk as the most notable cases and deaths of COVID-19 were found in the age range of seniors (typically aged 65 years or older). This is not a surprising fact considering that seniors are biologically more vulnerable to infections and death due to a weaker immune system and aging-related health conditions. Such conditions include high blood pressure, diabetes, cardiovascular diseases, cancer, and chronic diseases. These all serve to increase the risk that seniors have for COVID-19.

It is important to note that it is not just the physical ailments that hinders seniors' resilience to COVID-19, but also their mental health. Similar to physical issues related to aging, there is also a lowered mental health resilience among the elderly. Individuals 60 years or older are classified as more mentally vulnerable than any other age group (Lee et al., 2020). In a recent study conducted on the negative impact of COVID-19 on individuals, the elderly reported the greatest symptoms of anxiety, stress, and severe depression (Lee et al., 2020). As social isolation has been prolonged, mental health concerns have also increased among seniors. Although social distancing and isolation has proven effective in containing the spread of the diseases, it has had a profound negative effect on the mental health of elderly as they are the demographic group that has experienced the effects of social isolation more profoundly than any other age groups (Lee et al., 2020). Thus, more care and support needs to be provided towards the elderly as they are most at risk of mental and physical health issues. Numerous studies have also classified social isolation as a 'serious public health concern' for seniors due to the increased physical and mental risks they face compared to other age groups (Girdhar et al., 2020; Lee et al., 2020).

Out of all groups, it is the elderly that struggle the most to adapt to technological methods of staying connected. Lockdown has caused many people to be dismissed, suspended or require transitioning to remote work in addition to reduced hours. Therefore, many living care facilities have had to stop allowing families and friends from visiting the elderly in order to decrease the spread of the disease. But this means that many elderly have had most if not all of their social connections inaccessible to them. With many elderly choosing not to engage in technology and social media due to a lack of knowledge or personal preference, the quarantine only heightens the loneliness and negative emotions that they may experience in the face of this pandemic. Such emotions include fear, anger, loneliness, boredom, stress, and depression. Additionally, elderly that are living with their families may be more fortunate as they are not socially isolated from their families, thus helping to mitigate the stressors of this pandemic and quarantine on elderly (Girdhar et al., 2020). But the lockdown has affected all aspects of peoples' lives, and family roles, chores, and burdens are not exempt from such a change. So families that are living with seniors may have had to implement safety measures such as maintaining social distancing within the home in consideration of COVID symptoms or existing ailments of family members (Girdhar et al., 2020). This results in isolation of a social and psychological nature and may be a factor for decreasing mental health in the elderly living with families (Girdhar et al., 2020). The most common issues that people experience includes separation from loved ones, uncertainty and stress over their disease status, loss of freedom and boredom; these are all issues that are compounded by the lockdown (Girdhar et al., 2020).

Studies have taken place investigating methods to combat these issues faced by the elderly. Research has found that more support needs to be provided in helping the elderly maintain their communication with the outside world and especially with loved ones. According to Girdhar et al. (2020), there are 6 categories of interventions that needs to be addressed to mitigate the adverse effects of quarantining on the elderly: befriending interventions, psychological therapies, social facilitation interventions, leisure and skill development, health and social care provision, and pet therapy. Befriending interventions are a type of social intervention aiming at building new friendships while social facilitation interventions are settings that encourage social connections through technology or in-person contact (Girdhar et al., 2020). Leisure and skill development were activities that allowed for learning or expansion of existing skills such as gardening, computer and internet use, and also sports (Girdhar et al., 2020). All of these interventions and therapies work on creating and maintaining social contact as well as supporting their mental and cognitive health (Girdhar et al., 2020). This is quite important for elderly since they have a harder time maintaining their social contacts in addition to being more at risk for COVID-19. Another study that used digital techniques such as video calls and teleconferencing calls proved useful in alleviating loneliness, but there are also drawbacks to this method due to not all elderly having internet enabled devices and the fact that not all elderly are inclined to use the internet (Girdhar et al., 2020). Overall, it is paramount that more awareness and support is provided for the elderly as they are the age group that is often left behind in terms of thought and support. Elderly are one of the most vulnerable age groups alongside children and also have reduced mental and physical resilience thus requiring additional resources at times. More interventions need to be established so that elderly can maintain or at least increase their social contact with family and friends. Such interventions may include technologies and the internet, but most importantly requires the coordination of health care workers, volunteers, and community outreach to ensure that the elderly are getting the necessary support needed to maintain their wellbeing.

The Effects of COVID 19 on Mental Health for the Impoverished

The start of the lockdown for COVID-19 meant major changes applied to all aspects of life, ranging from the workplace to lifestyle and home. The majority of people working in industries such as finance, educational, professional, scientific, and technical services were able to transition to working from home or teleworking (Deng et al., 2020). But jobs in industries requiring hands-on application such as food services, agriculture, forestry, fishing, hunting, health care, transportation and warehousing are unable to transition to teleworking or working from home (Deng et al., 2020). Minimum wage jobs often fall within the latter category. Thus, many low income households that may already be enduring financial struggles and hardships have their financial difficulties compounded by their work situations (Team & Manderson, 2020). These workers may also be under more stress about the potential dangers that they may face while working their job, along with the danger they may pose to their family members that may be more at risk (Team & Manderson, 2020). The disparity in income between industries with low teleworking possibilities and those with high teleworking possibilities means that many workers living under the poverty line or working minimum wage jobs are at higher risk of the pandemic negatively impacting their mental health. Furthermore, because not all workplaces offer remote work, many minimum wage workers may face a reduction in their hours or greater struggles in finding transportation to work (as transportation is also affected). These issues all compound the mental health issues that some may be facing and may make them more susceptible to COVID-19 (Team & Manderson, 2020). Although many governments have provided relief funds in relation to COVID-19, it still may not be sufficient for some households depending on the amount and frequency of such funds. Furthermore, these funds may provide financial relief for workers, but many may still suffer from mental health issues that require time and money. This tends to not be the case for those with a middle or high income who are more likely to possess a monetary safety net alleviating some stress over their financial situation (Team & Manderson, 2020). Therefore, in the event that a high income worker is unable to retain their job or have suffered reduced work hours, they are not as severely impacted as minimum wage workers. Furthermore, many high income workers with reduced work hours or telework now have more control over their daily schedules, a luxury that is often not afforded to impoverished or low income households.

Conclusion

Overall, this chapter explores the various ways in which the elderly are more at risk in terms of mental and physical health in terms of the lack of support and the additional ways support can be provided. It explores the struggles that the elderly face in maintaining their social connections and the effects of lockdown on these connections. Furthermore, suggestions are made on interventions that can be implemented to support the elderly and maintain their social bonds, which possess long-term and short-term benefits. In addition, the disparity between minimum wage workers and middle to high income workers in terms is discussed in relation to the various ways their mental health is affected by COVID-19. Minimum wage workers tend to experience a greater negative effect on their mental health while many middle to high income workers are able to experience greater control over their jobs and alleviate mental stress related to their everyday life or COVID-19. Although high income workers may face the same stressors as low income workers with regards to the pandemic, they have greater amounts of resources and control over their situation that low income workers do not have access to. Though this pandemic has led to an exponential increase in research conducted on the effects of COVID-19, social isolation, and support provided, there needs to be greater awareness of the issues that the elderly face along with increased efforts to provide support to low income individuals, as they are one of the most affected groups. This pandemic has impacted every aspect of life and caused much evaluation to be made in regards to the support, or lack of, provided to the elderly along with other marginalized groups. It is important to recognize the growing need for support and services to help protect the most vulnerable of society.

Chapter 7:

The Implications
of
Teletherapy During COVID-19

Shannon Lin

Introduction

In March 2020, the World Health Organization declared the coronavirus (COVID-19) outbreak a pandemic (Burgoyne & Cohn, 2020; WHO 2020, as cited in Sampaio et al., 2021). COVID-19 has since presented a multitude of challenges surrounding mental health and mental health care, to say the least (Moring et al., 2020; CDC, 2020, as cited in Sampaio et al., 2021; Sun et al., 2020). As mental health therapists are considered to be frontline essential workers, it is especially important for psychology patients to continue to receive clinical therapy during the crisis despite minimal training and preparation for remote therapy on the practitioner's end (Bashshur et al., 2020; Moring et al., 2020; CDC, 2020, as cited in Sampaio et al., 2021). Following the literature review on mental health and remote treatment during COVID-19 through the perspectives of the patient and practitioner, this chapter will conclude with an interview with a fellow peer of the author, which will provide first-hand experience on remote therapy during the COVID-19 pandemic. It is important to recognize the challenges and significance of remote therapy during a global health crisis, as this indicates the potentials and drawbacks of technology at a time when it is needed more than ever.

T is for Teletherapy

According to Burgoyne and Cohn (2020), the practice of teletherapy is not considered new. Also referred to as telehealth, telemedicine, telepsychology, telepsychotherapy, telemental health, or telepsychiatry, teletherapy is predicted to rapidly evolve with the increasing dependence on electronic technologies that are prevalent in all sectors of society (Bashshur et al., 2020; Burgoyne & Cohn, 2020; Moring et al., 2020). This increasing reliance on technology is exemplified throughout the education, commerce, transportation, entertainment, and communications industries, and the use of health services delivered via communication technologies is now no longer a stranger to us (Bashshur et al., 2020; Burgoyne & Cohn, 2020; Brown, 2017, as cited in Moring et al., 2020; Sampaio et al., 2021). While it was initially implemented to increase accessibility to mental health professionals outside a clinical setting for populations in rural areas, some teletherapy services have been present since 2006, where the China American Psychoanalytic Alliance (CAPA) has since delivered psychoanalytic psychotherapy entirely over the internet (Fortney et al., 2020 and Hassija & Gray, 2011, as cited in Moring et al., 2020; Wang et al., 2021). Other services that have emerged over the years include BetterHelp, Talkspace, and Regain, which utilize live chat, text, phone, and video chat technologies (Burgoyne & Cohn, 2020). These advantages to accessibility are shown to benefit consumers such as rural, disabled, and housebound clients (Burgoyne & Cohn, 2020). Although therapists and the public alike have displayed skepticism toward the practice of teletherapy, nonetheless, it is found to be a trustworthy option of mental health treatment with promising results and good user satisfaction (Burgoyne & Cohn, 2020; Wang et al., 2021). Thus, it is important to evaluate the unique opportunities, considerations, and challenges that arise when technology and psychological services are merged, especially with the sudden onset of the COVID-19 pandemic in early 2020 (American Psychological Association, 2013, as cited in Sampaio et al., 2021).

The Onset of COVID-19 and the Shift to Teletherapy

In March 2020, the World Health Organization (WHO) officially declared COVID-19 a pandemic (Burgoyne & Cohn, 2020; WHO 2020, as cited in Sampaio et al., 2021). Within a few short months, COVID-19 fled into over 200 countries, infected more than 3 million people, and took the lives of over 239,000 (Sun et al., 2020). As frontline essential workers, therapists found themselves rethinking and adapting to how they would provide care with minimal training, planning, or preparation (Bashshur et al., 2020; Moring et al., 2020; Sampaio et al., 2021). During a global health crisis such as COVID-19, the American Psychological Association (APA) Ethics Code states that "therapists have an ethical responsibility to continue helping their clients, colleagues, and trainees, and to do no harm" (Chenneville & Schwartz-Mette, 2020, as cited in Sampaio et al., 2021, p. 12). In response to the need to protect others from infection and adhere to the isolation mandates, teletherapy quickly became a primary method of service delivery as a substitute for in-person care (Bashshur et al., 2020; Burgoyne & Cohn, 2020; Moring et al., 2020, Wang et al., 2021). As a result, technology became a vital necessity for mental health service providers to connect and meet the needs of individuals, and ensure continuity of care (Burgoyne & Cohn, 2020; Moring et al., 2020; Wang et al., 2021). Therapists are increasing their usage of telecommunication modes such as phone, email, and texting, whereas video conferencing platforms such as Zoom, Facetime, and Google Hangouts continue to increase in popularity (Osei-Buapim, 2021; Sampaio et al., 2021).

This transformed flow of information between the therapist and client therefore must be sustained effectively during a global pandemic (Burgoyne & Cohn, 2020). Through teletherapy, therapists must consider the onset of issues that have become more explicit due to the pandemic. For example, the rapid rise of intimate partner violence cases during COVID-19 has created a cause for concern regarding the safety and privacy of a client when using teletherapy, compared to a physical office that provides a place of refuge from possible violence (Bosman, 2020 and Campbell, 2020, as cited in Burgoyne & Cohn, 2020). Additionally, there is no doubt that COVID-19 has, unfortunately, led to a high number of deaths that leave the grieving with increased needs for mental health care (Sun et al., 2020). This can occur from a multitude of events, such as the inability to comfort or care for ill family members or dying loved ones, which increase feelings of grief, distress, and guilt (Sun et al., 2020). Some individuals may experience unremitting or disabling mourning, which manifests through physical and psychological effects including depression, post-traumatic stress disorder, and complicated grief (Sun et al., 2020). These effects can be exacerbated in disadvantaged populations and those with previous mental health problems, where a low socioeconomic status, lack of social support, and lack of economic resources can increase the vulnerability of those who are grieving (Sun et al., 2020). While the unpredictable nature of the pandemic can also induce an increase in stress, fear, and anxiety, individuals who have pre-existing mental health conditions such as depression, schizophrenia, or substance use disorders can potentially exhibit unusually strong reactions to a crisis situation like COVID-19 (Moring et al., 2020; CDC, 2020, as cited in Sampaio et al., 2021). For others, a crisis situation may exacerbate a patient's psychological symptoms (Sampaio et al., 2021). COVID-19 has further divided this accessibility to therapy services through increased unemployment rates and insurance benefit losses, which demonstrates how "traumatic or sudden loss during public health emergencies ... can be more detrimental and harder to resolve than natural or less sudden losses" (Sampaio et al., 2021; Sun et al., 2020).

Teletherapy from the Patient's Perspective

Several studies conclude that teletherapy is an effective mode of treatment with several additional benefits, both COVID-19 and non-COVID-19 related (Burgoyne & Cohn, 2020; Moring et al., 2020; Osei-Buapim, 2021). Largely, the convenience of teletherapy bypasses several barriers that may create difficulties or challenges to access therapy for many individuals (Bashshur et al., 2020; Moring et al., 2020). In addition to infection risk avoidance, teletherapy services during the COVID-19 pandemic allows individuals who once required additional time and costs associated with travel to access mental health treatment, especially with limited local availability of treatment, as well as those with who have time constraints due to work and family commitments (Bashshur et al., 2020; Brown, 2017 and Kazdin & Blasé, 2011, as cited in Moring et al., 2020). One important finding is that teletherapy is beneficial for removing the perceived stigma that is associated with receiving mental health care in-person (Greene-Shortridge et al., 2007, as cited in Moring et al., 2020; Sun et al., 2020). Osei-Buapim (2021) finds that for some, the phone provides a psychological defense mechanism against the anxieties and discomforts that manifest when talking about thoughts, feelings, and past experiences in person. This establishes a newfound dimension of a safe space for patients to express themselves and feel more safe.

As teletherapy became an essential and safe mode of mental health therapy during the wake of COVID-19, it is shown to be well-respected by patients who receive various types of treatment (Moring et al., 2020). In an article on delivering cognitive processing therapy (CPT) via teletherapy by Moring and colleagues (2020), the authors reassure that the efficacy of CPT is not compromised through teletherapy. Through several uncontrolled and randomized controlled studies that compare the outcomes of in-person therapy and teletherapy, CPT delivered via teletherapy is shown to significantly reduce post-traumatic stress disorder (PTSD) symptoms, demonstrating its efficacy and noninferiority to in-person methodologies (Moring et al., 2020). Burgoyne and Cohn (2020) express that youths and teenagers respond well to teletherapy with shorter and frequent sessions, while the flexibility of teletherapy becomes more feasible for family work due to fewer time constraints and distance. In family work, teletherapy also enables therapists to see the family within their living space (Burgoyne & Cohn, 2020).

Through a patient's perspective, there are also some downfalls of teletherapy that one must anticipate. Several studies discuss the concerns regarding privacy and confidentiality when receiving teletherapy (Burgoyne & Cohn, 2020; Osei-Buapim, 2021; Sampaio et al., 2021). As COVID-19 has forced mental health care outside of a structured office space into an online one, individuals who live with other family members find obtaining a sense of privacy to be quite challenging (Burgoyne & Cohn, 2020; Sampaio et al., 2021). For adolescents and teenagers who typically associate the online space as a means of socializing, this transition is considered to be more awkward or anxiety provoking at times (Burgoyne & Cohn, 2020). It is important to acknowledge that any treatment approach must create a safe space for adolescents to express themselves and their anxieties, which can become problematic if parents struggle to respect these requests by the adolescent's therapist, or if they are unable to obtain privacy due to certain family dynamics (Burgoyne & Cohn, 2020; Osei-Buapim, 2021). With this loss of a physical presence that conventional in-person treatment offers, teletherapy also raises additional privacy concerns in an online space related to client confidentiality (Burgoyne & Cohn, 2020; Osei-Buapim, 2021). On both ends of providing and receiving therapy via telecommunicative means, patients and therapists alike are more vulnerable to hackers and having personal, identifiable information leaked (Strauss, 2020 and Wilson, 2011, as cited in Osei-Buapim, 2021). As platforms such as Zoom gain popularity and suffer from events like a hack, greater precautions and vigilance must be considered when dealing with the exchange of sensitive information (Osei-Buapim, 2021).

Teletherapy from the Practitioner's Perspective

Similarly, therapists have experienced a great length of struggles and challenges when navigating teletherapy during COVID-19 (Sampaio et al., 2021). During the transition, issues surrounding an unfamiliarity with technology and a lack of training (and training opportunities) for conducting telecommunication services became paramount (Bashshur et al., 2020; Sampaio et al., 2021; Wang et al., 2021). At times, technology alone can become problematic as therapy sessions require a functioning and well-maintained equipment and networks (Bashshur et al., 2020). As a result, this can potentially reduce the effectiveness of psychotherapy (Wang et al., 2021). Additional challenges that surface through teletherapy largely relate to the feedback and nonverbal cues that therapists are trained to discern during in-person sessions (Burgoyne & Cohn, 2020; Moring et al., 2020). In therapy, feedback is considered to be an informative response to the treatment plan via nonverbal behaviours and facial expressions (Burgoyne & Cohn, 2020). The quantity and quality of feedback is compromised and is far more limited in teletherapy as it is impacted by the technology and equipment that is used by each party (Burgoyne & Cohn, 2020). Furthermore, Gros et al. (2013) in the article by Moring and colleagues (2020) point out that in teletherapy, therapists have a harder time identifying or responding to clients who may be intoxicated or high. In this online space, a loss of immediate cues can easily inhibit a provider from picking up cues that indicate the influence of alcohol or drugs (Moring et al., 2020). This is important to recognize as the majority of the surveyed practitioners in the study by Sampaio and colleagues (2021) report having inadequate or insufficient skills to manage emergency situations through online counseling modes.

For providers of children and school-aged clients, the transition to teletherapy due to COVID-19 has not been an easy feat either. To keep children engaged during teletherapy, therapists often had to introduce new plans and strategies for each client and session (Burgoyne & Cohn, 2020). For some, teletherapy for children would oftentimes feel like a babysitting service for parents who struggle with time, instead of providing therapy work (Sampaio et al., 2021). Osei-Buapim (2021) states that for student patients, the therapeutic relationship is crucial to sustaining continued treatment in a remote therapy situation. A therapeutic relationship that is usually established through in-person treatment can easily become impersonal in teletherapy, where the physical distance can be mirrored with an emotional distance (Osei-Buapim, 2021). During COVID-19, this became apparent through regressed behaviours and expressions of agitation in student clients (Osei-Buapim, 2021). In remote therapy, this is demonstrated through feelings of intrusion as the therapists called the students through their

cell phones, eliciting a stoic affect or refusal to engage in therapy
(Osei-Buapim, 2021).

The APA Ethics Code that encourages psychologists to practice
flexibility in emergency situations also creates an ethical dilemma for
therapists during COVID-19 (Sampaio et al., 2021). With an ethical
obligation to continue their care for patients during a worldwide major
crisis, the need for mental health care is heightened as many patients
have more psychological troubles and symptoms than usual (Sampaio
et al., 2021). As frontline workers, this role becomes more stressful and
demanding when factoring in the rapid role shifting and distractions
that come with working from home (Burgoyne & Cohn, 2020; Sampaio
et al., 2021). In a survey of 768 English-speaking mental health
professionals regarding the adaptation of teletherapy during COVID-19
by Sampaio and colleagues (2021), the results indicate that most
participants need to receive more training and education on the technical
aspects of delivering teletherapy. With higher than usual difficulties
during the pandemic due to the combined stresses of technology and
increased demands for care, the results also report elevated rates of
burnout experienced by therapists (Sampaio et al., 2021). Defined as a
"state of mental and physical exhaustion caused by one's professional
life," COVID-19 aggravates this outcome as therapists deal with their
own difficulties and fears during isolation, as well as the anxieties that
the pandemic elicits (Freudenberger, 1974, as cited in Sampaio

et al., 2021, p. 12).

Teletherapy During COVID-19:
A Personal Interview

The above points regarding teletherapy during COVID-19 can be
demonstrated through a personal interview with a fellow peer of the
author, who wishes to remain anonymous. To be discussed further in
the following section, the interviewee has had previous experience with

in-person treatments prior to COVID-19, and began remote treatment with a different therapist during the wake of COVID-19 in the spring of 2020 (Anonymous, personal communication, August 22, 2021). Treatment was originally pursued to assist with major depressive disorder (dysmythia) and anxiety, which the interviewee has dealt with for over ten years. As opposed to a public health service, the therapist that the interviewee sought was provided privately, which indicated that the patient's files and information were not easily transferable. Despite the challenges that were brought forth from transitioning to another practitioner, the prevalence of teletherapy provided a vast array of therapy options for the interviewee to select from and refer to. One unique circumstance that the interviewee experienced was an abrupt ending to the sessions, which was unexpected. This occurred due to additional obligations assigned to the practitioner, which left them unavailable to continue care for patients. While the interviewee stated that a lot of progress was made during therapy through opening up with trauma and navigating depression and anxiety with the practitioner, this sudden stop in mental health care was ultimately, unexpected and unprepared for.A series of questions regarding the impact of COVID-19 on mental health and teletherapy were posed to the interviewee by the author. These questions encompassed various sets of topics, including the impact of COVID-19 on mental health, the advantages and disadvantages of teletherapy, how well the therapist adapted to teletherapy, the differences between in-person and remote treatment, as well as concerns regarding privacy. Firstly, the question of whether COVID-19 brought forth a worsening onset of mental health symptoms or conditions was addressed. Like the findings by Sun et al. (2020), the interviewee suggested that the pandemic was difficult to deal with, especially when underlying symptoms are present and become exacerbated. The isolation mandates, when placed on an immunocompromised individual who lives alone, forces one to be "stuck alone with emotions a lot more."

In hopes of receiving quality mental health care during a global health crisis, the interviewee was fortunate enough to find a practitioner who was overall well prepared for teletherapy. The therapist was able to stay focused during each session within an enclosed space and minimal distractions. Through slideshows and visual prompts that were prepared for each session, the interviewee also appreciated the homework that was assigned after each session as an incentive to stay on track and make progress. Such tasks included going outside for thirty minutes every day, or writing in a journal, which were at times shared with the practitioner in confidence. After their treatments ended, the interviewee expressed that not having a scheduled session every week to discuss the homework with someone made them lose the motivation to practice the given exercises.

Despite the efforts to stay well prepared and well equipped, however, the interviewee reflected on how technological issues can easily "throw off your whole day" due to cancelled or delayed appointments. Like several studies have pointed out, access to the Internet and modern technologies are essential for teletherapy, as Internet or power issues can provoke challenges when individuals devote a certain time to intimately express and exchange feelings (Burgoyne & Cohn, 2020; Moring et al., 2020; Wang et al., 2021). While an audio call may suffice for disruptions in video conferencing, the interviewee described this to feel less personal as there is no face attributed to the voice.

Showing up and being present in a treatment session is considered to be an accomplishment in and of itself, which the interviewee emphasized. When having to travel to an in-person appointment, the interviewee explains that doing so can be a difficult ordeal, while calling to cancel an in-person appointment is much easier to do instead. Without the need to commute or leave their place of residence, the interviewee expressed that therapy was "easier to show up to when it was online," but also pointed out that having an in-person session provides an opportunity for one to leave their home and have something (an event) to accomplish for that day. Through this experience and realization, the interviewee found themselves more willing to do in-person sessions after trying teletherapy.

"If you don't live alone, there is little privacy." From this statement, the interviewee highlighted that having people around can impact what is said during therapy, and suggested that privacy can be achieved through relocating to a car or a private, outdoor space, which can replicate the feeling of "being really alone so you can share like someone is right next to you." When discussing the preference for video or audio calls, the interviewee described a higher level of intimacy to be achieved through video calls, which was a requirement of the therapist. While it was at first intimidating as the interviewee did not like their face shown on camera, this heightened ability for the therapist to read their body language (and vice versa) were found to be an essential element to making treatment progress. Video calls also allowed the interviewee to "build a better relationship with that person [the therapist] when you can see them throughout the whole time." Despite these advantages, the interviewee also identified a huge drawback to remote therapy methods, as emotions may be expressed more discreetly (i.e. crying), and there may be undetected activities off-screen (i.e. fidgeting hands under the table) that are far more difficult to read by the therapist.

Through in-person therapy, the interviewee described the experience to allow "you to get to know each other better and intimately" compared to teletherapy, where "you know it is real but there is a slight removal or feeling of withdrawnness because they are not physically in front of you." Using online classroom peers as an analogy for this, the degree of vulnerability via remote therapy methods is therefore shifted. Through virtual methodologies, the interviewee found that "you are able to get comfortable with sharing with a therapist through that wall, which is talking to a screen." When the sense of a therapeutic relationship is removed, "you don't know the person as much since they are online, so I can share a lot and what I say doesn't matter as much." One factor that did impact what was shared with the therapist was the fact that the interviewee gave consent at the beginning of selected sessions for the therapist to record for the supervisor to review, which "changes everything." As the interviewee did not know who the supervisor was, being video recorded brought on a sense of caution for the interviewee to be less willing to share secrets and be less open and vulnerable. Overall, this experience of teletherapy during COVID-19 demonstrates the importance of trust within a therapeutic relationship, as well as the heavy reliance on technology to make the experience feel as real and in-person as possible.

Concluding Thoughts

Teletherapy during COVID-19 has indeed become an essential and integral mode of mental health treatment in order to protect others from infection and establish safe isolation practices (Bashshur et al., 2020; Burgoyne & Cohn, 2020; Moring et al., 2020; Wang et al., 2021). While the positive responses on teletherapy are plentiful, including the convenience and ease of accessibility for many patients, this transition has overall been more demanding than not for mental health practitioners (Bashshur et al., 2020; Burgoyne & Cohn, 2020; Moring et al., 2020; Osei-Buapim, 2021; Sampaio et al., 2021; Wang et al., 2021). As therapists juggle this ethical dilemma and obligation to continue care for clients, including the rise in psychological troubles and symptoms during the pandemic, they also have to deal with their own personal and professional struggles, which eventually manifests as burnout (Burgoyne & Cohn, 2020; Sampaio et al., 2021; Sun et al., 2020). Concerns regarding feedback and privacy are impacted through teletherapy as well, which must be taken into consideration when moving forward with teletherapy practices (Burgoyne & Cohn, 2020; Moring et al., 2020;

Osei-Baupim, 2021; Sampaio et al., 2021). Through various studies and a personal interview that provide several perspectives on teletherapy during the COVID-19 pandemic, teletherapy has been shown to create a remarkable impact on the quality of mental health care for both patients and practitioners alike.

References

Chapter 1

References

Cao, W., Fang, Z., Hou, G., Han, M., Xu, X., Dong, J., & Zheng, J. (2020). The psychological impact of the COVID-19 epidemic on college students in China. *Psychiatry research, 287,* 112934.

Marroquín, B., Vine, V., & Morgan, R. (2020). Mental health during the COVID-19 pandemic: Effects of stay-at-home policies, social distancing behavior, and social resources. *Psychiatry research, 293,* 113419.

Tull, M. T., Edmonds, K. A., Scamaldo, K. M., Richmond, J. R., Rose, J. P., & Gratz, K. L. (2020). Psychological outcomes associated with stay-at-home orders and the perceived impact of COVID-19 on daily life. *Psychiatry research, 289,* 113098.

Chapter 2

References

Alam, S. B., Willows, S., Kulka, M., & Sandhu, J. K. (2020). Severe acute respiratory syndrome coronavirus 2 may be an underappreciated pathogen of the central nervous system. *European Journal of Neurology, 27*(11), 2348–2360. https://doi.org/10.1111/ene.14442

Butowt, R., & von Bartheld, C. S. (2020). Anosmia in COVID-19: Underlying Mechanisms and Assessment of an Olfactory Route to Brain Infection. *The Neuroscientist*, 107385842095690. doi:10.1177/1073858420956905

Kohli, P., Soler, Z. M., Nguyen, S. A., Muus, J. S., & Schlosser, R. J. (2016). The Association Between Olfaction and Depression: A Systematic Review. *Chemical Senses, 41*(6), 479–486. https://doi.org/10.1093/chemse/bjw061

Li, Y., Fu, L., Gonzales, D. M., & Lavi, E. (2004). Coronavirus Neurovirulence Correlates with the Ability of the Virus To Induce Proinflammatory Cytokine Signals from Astrocytes and Microglia. *Journal of Virology, 78*(7), 3398–3406. doi:10.1128/jvi.78.7.3398-3406.2004

Li, H., Xue, Q., & Xu, X. (2020). Involvement of the Nervous System in SARS-CoV-2 Infection. *Neurotoxicity Research, 38*, 1–7. doi:10.1007/s12640-020-00219-8

Mao, L., Jin, H., Wang, M., Hu, Y., Chen, S., He, Q., … Hu, B. (2020). Neurologic Manifestations of Hospitalized Patients With Coronavirus Disease 2019 in Wuhan, China. *JAMA Neurology, 77*(6), 683–690. doi:10.1001/jamaneurol.2020.1127

Morales-Medina, J. C., Iannitti, T., Freeman, A., & Caldwell, H. K. (2017). The olfactory bulbectomized rat as a model of depression: The hippocampal pathway. *Behavioural Brain Research, 317*, 562–575. doi:10.1016/j.bbr.2016.09.029

Sfera, A., Osorio, C., Price, A. I., Gradini, R., & Cummings, M. (2015). Delirium from the gliocentric perspective. *Frontiers in Cellular Neuroscience, 9*(171). https://doi.org/10.3389/fncel.2015.00171

Tsuruta, R., & Oda, Y. (2016). A clinical perspective of sepsis-associated delirium. *Journal of intensive care, 4*(18). https://doi.org/10.1186/s40560-016-0145-4

Vargas, G., Medeiros Geraldo, L. H., Salomão, N., Paes, M. V., Souza Lima, F. R., & Alcantara Gomes, F. C. (2020). Severe Acute Respiratory Syndrome Coronavirus 2 (SARS-CoV-2) and Glial Cells: insights and perspectives. *Brain, Behavior, & Immunity - Health, 7,* 100127. doi:10.1016/j.bbih.2020.100127

Yom-Tov, E., Lekkas, D., & Jacobson, N. C. (2021). Association of COVID19-induced anosmia and ageusia with depression and suicidal ideation. *Journal of Affective Disorders Reports, 5,* 100156. https://doi.org/10.1016/j.jadr.2021.100156

Chapter 3

References

Banerjee, D., Kosagisharaf, J. R., & Sathyanarayana Rao, T. S. (2021). 'The dual PANDEMIC' of suicide and covid-19: A BIOPSYCHOSOCIAL narrative of risks and prevention. *Psychiatry Research, 295,* 113577. https://doi.org/10.1016/j.psychres.2020.113577

Bhavsar, V., Kirkpatrick, K., Calcia, M., & Howard, L. M. (2021). Lockdown, domestic abuse perpetration, and mental health care: Gaps in training, research, and policy. *The Lancet Psychiatry, 8*(3), 172–174. https://doi.org/10.1016/s2215-0366(20)30397-7

BOLT Safety Society. (2021, February 3). *How has the COVID-19 pandemic affected the domestic abuse crisis? | Episode 8 | Backyards with Bolt* [Video]. YouTube. https://youtu.be/AJztv-CAreg

Hegarty, K., & Roberts, G. (1998). How common is domestic violence against women? The definition of partner abuse in prevalence studies. *Australian and New Zealand Journal of Public Health, 22*(1), 49–54. https://doi.org/10.1111/j.1467-842x.1998.tb01144.x

Mechanic, M. B., Weaver, T. L., & Resick, P. A. (2008). Mental health consequences of intimate partner abuse. *Violence Against Women, 14*(6),

634–654. https://doi.org/10.1177/1077801208319283

Norwood, A., & Murphy, C. (2012). What forms of abuse correlate with ptsd symptoms in partners of men being treated for intimate partner violence? *Psychological Trauma: Theory, Research, Practice, and Policy, 4*(6), 596–604. https://doi.org/10.1037/a0025232

Renwick, N. (2002). The 'nameless fever': The HIV/AIDS pandemic and China's women. *Third World Quarterly, 23*(2), 377–393. https://doi.org/10.1080/01436590220126694

Sackett, L. A., & Saunders,, D. G. (1999). The impact of different forms of psychological abuse on battered women. *Violence and Victims, 14*(1), 105–117. https://doi.org/10.1891/0886-6708.14.1.105

Trevillion, K., Howard, L. M., Morgan, C., Feder, G., Woodall, A., & Rose, D. (2012). The response of mental health services to domestic violence. *Journal of the American Psychiatric Nurses Association, 18*(6), 326–336. https://doi.org/10.1177/1078390312459747

Wilson, K. J. (2005). *When violence begins at home: A comprehensive guide to understanding and ending domestic abuse.* Hunter House.

Chapter 4

References

Son, C., Hegde, S., Smith, A., Wang, X., & Sasangohar, F. (2020). Effects of covid-19 on College Students' mental health in the United States: INTERVIEW survey study. *Journal of Medical Internet Research, 22*(9). https://doi.org/10.2196/21279

Lee, J., Solomon, M., Stead, T., Kwon, B., & Ganti, L. (2021). Impact of covid-19 on the mental health of US college students. *BMC Psychology, 9*(1). https://doi.org/10.1186/s40359-021-00598-3

Browning, M. H., Larson, L. R., Sharaievska, I., Rigolon, A., McAnirlin, O., Mullenbach, L., Cloutier, S., Vu, T. M., Thomsen, J., Reigner, N., Metcalf, E. C., D'Antonio, A., Helbich, M., Bratman, G. N., & Alvarez, H. O. (2021). Psychological impacts FROM COVID-19 among UNIVERSITY STUDENTS: Risk factors across seven states in the United States. *PLOS ONE*, *16*(1). https://doi.org/10.1371/journal.pone.0245327

Cao, W., Fang, Z., Hou, G., Han, M., Xu, X., Dong, J., & Zheng, J. (2020). The psychological impact of the COVID-19 epidemic on college students in China. *Psychiatry Research*, *287*, 112934. https://doi.org/10.1016/j.psychres.2020.112934

 Sampaio, F., Sequeira, C., & Teixeira, L. (2021). Impact of COVID-19 outbreak On nurses' mental Health: A prospective cohort study. *Environmental Research*, *194*, 110620. https://doi.org/10.1016/j.envres.2020.110620

An, Y., Yang, Y., Wang, A., Li, Y., Zhang, Q., Cheung, T., Ungvari, G. S., Qin, M. Z., An, F. R., & Xiang, Y. T. (2020). Prevalence of depression and its impact on quality of life among frontline nurses in emergency departments during the COVID-19 outbreak. *Journal of affective disorders*, *276*, 312–315. https://doi.org/10.1016/j.jad.2020.06.047

Spoorthy, M. S., Pratapa, S. K., & Mahant, S. (2020). Mental health problems faced by healthcare workers due to the Covid-19 Pandemic–a review. *Asian Journal of Psychiatry*, *51*, 102119. https://doi.org/10.1016/j.ajp.2020.102119

Chapter 5

References

Alikhani, R., Salimi, A., Hormati, A., & Aminnejad, R. (2020). Mental health advice for frontline healthcare providers caring for patients with COVID-19. In *Canadian Journal of Anesthesia* (Vol. 67, Issue 8). https://doi.org/10.1007/s12630-020-01650-3

Braquehais, M. D., Vargas-Cáceres, S., Gómez-Durán, E., Nieva, G., Valero, S., Casas, M., & Bruguera, E. (2020a). The impact of the COVID-19 pandemic on the mental health of healthcare professionals. In *QJM* (Vol. 113, Issue 9). https://doi.org/10.1093/qjmed/hcaa207

Braquehais, M. D., Vargas-Cáceres, S., Gómez-Durán, E., Nieva, G., Valero, S., Casas, M., & Bruguera, E. (2020b). The impact of the COVID-19 pandemic on the mental health of healthcare professionals. In *QJM* (Vol. 113, Issue 9). https://doi.org/10.1093/qjmed/hcaa207

Comfort, A. B., Krezanoski, P. J., Rao, L., el Ayadi, A., Tsai, A. C., Goodman, S., & Harper, C. C. (2021). Mental health among outpatient reproductive health care providers during the US COVID-19 epidemic. *Reproductive Health*, *18*(1). https://doi.org/10.1186/s12978-021-01102-1

di Tella, M., Romeo, A., Benfante, A., & Castelli, L. (2020). Mental health of healthcare workers during the COVID-19 pandemic in Italy. *Journal of Evaluation in Clinical Practice*, *26*(6). https://doi.org/10.1111/jep.13444

Eftekhar Ardebili, M., Naserbakht, M., Bernstein, C., Alazmani-Noodeh, F., Hakimi, H., & Ranjbar, H. (2021). Healthcare providers experience of working during the COVID-19 pandemic: A qualitative study. *American Journal of Infection Control*, *49*(5). https://doi.org/10.1016/j.ajic.2020.10.001

Kumar, A., & Nayar, K. R. (2020). COVID 19 and its mental health consequences. In *Journal of Mental Health*. https://doi.org/10.1080/09638237.2020.1757052

Mi, T., Yang, X., Sun, S., Li, X., Tam, C. C., Zhou, Y., & Shen, Z. (2021). Mental Health Problems of HIV Healthcare Providers During the COVID-19 Pandemic: The Interactive Effects of Stressors and Coping. *AIDS and Behavior*, *25*(1). https://doi.org/10.1007/s10461-020-03073-z

Ornell, F., Halpern, S. C., Kessler, F. H. P., & Narvaez, J. C. D. M. (2020). The impact of the COVID-19 pandemic on the mental health of healthcare professionals. *Cadernos de Saúde Pública*, *36*(4). https://doi.org/10.1590/0102-311x00063520

Pearman, A., Hughes, M. L., Smith, E. L., & Neupert, S. D. (2020). Mental Health Challenges of United States Healthcare Professionals During COVID-19. *Frontiers in Psychology*, *11*. https://doi.org/10.3389/fpsyg.2020.02065

Slone, H., Gutierrez, A., Lutzky, C., Zhu, D., Hedriana, H., Barrera, J. F., Paige, S. R., & Bunnell, B. E. (2021). Assessing the impact of COVID-19 on mental health providers in the southeastern United States. *Psychiatry Research*, *302*. https://doi.org/10.1016/j.psychres.2021.114055

Sultana, A., Sharma, R., Hossain, M. M., Bhattacharya, S., & Purohit, N. (2020). Burnout among healthcare providers during COVID-19: Challenges and evidence-based interventions. *Indian Journal of Medical Ethics*, *V*(4). https://doi.org/10.20529/IJME.2020.73

Vizheh, M., Qorbani, M., Arzaghi, S. M., Muhidin, S., Javanmard, Z., & Esmaeili, M. (2020). The mental health of healthcare workers in the COVID-19 pandemic: A systematic review. In *Journal of Diabetes and Metabolic Disorders* (Vol. 19, Issue 2). https://doi.org/10.1007/s40200-020-00643-9

Chapter 6

References

Deng, Z., Morissette, R., & Messacar, D. (2020). Running the economy remotely: Potential for working from home during and after COVID-19. Statistics Canada, Catalogue no.45280001. https://www150.statcan.gc.ca/n1/en/pub/45-28-0001/2020001/article/00026-eng.pdf? st=ush4vDO-

Girdhar, R., Srivastava, V., & Sethi, S. (2020). Managing mental health issues among elderly during COVID-19 pandemic. *J Geriatr Care Res*, 7(1), 32-35.

Lee, K., Jeong, G., & Yim, J. E. (2020). Consideration of the psychological and mental health of the elderly during COVID-19: A theoretical review. *Int. J. Environ. Res. Public Health*,

17(21), 8098. https://doi.org/10.3390/ijerph17218098.

Team, V., & Manderson, L. (2020). How COVID-19 reveals structures of vulnerability. *Med Anthropol*, *39*(8), 671-674. 10.1080/01459740.2020.1830281

Chapter 7

References

Bashshur, R. L., Doarn, C. R., Frenk, J. M., Kvedar, J. C., Shannon, G. W., & Woolliscroft, J. O. (2020). Beyond the COVID pandemic, telemedicine, and health care. *Telemedicine Journal and e-Health*, *26*(11), 1310–1312. https://doi.org/10.1089/tmj.2020.0328

Burgoyne, N., & Cohn, A. S. (2020). Lessons from the transition to relational teletherapy during COVID-19. *Family Process*, *59*(3), 974–984. https://doi.org/10.1111/famp.12589

Moring, J. C., Dondanville, K. A., Fina, B. A., Hassija, C., Chard, K., Monson, C., LoSavio, S. T., Wells, S. Y., Morland, L. A., Kaysen, D., Galovski, T. E., & Resick, P. A. (2020). Cognitive processing therapy for posttraumatic stress disorder via telehealth: Practical considerations during the COVID-19 pandemic. *Journal of Traumatic Stress*, *33*(4), 371–377. https://doi.org/10.1002/jts.22544

Osei-Buapim, C. (2021). Transition to teletherapy with adolescents in the wake of the COVID-19 pandemic: The holding environment approach. In C. Tosone (Eds.), *Shared Trauma, Shared Resilience During a Pandemic* (1st ed., pp. 146-153). New York, NY: Springer. Retrieved from https://link-springer-com.proxy.lib.sfu.ca/content/pdf/10.1007%2F978-3-030-61442-3.pdf

Sampaio, M., Haro, M. V. N., De Sousa, B., Melo, W. V., & Hoffman, H. G. (2021). Therapists make the switch to telepsychology to safely continue treating their patients during the COVID-19 pandemic. Virtual reality telepsychology may be next. *Frontiers in Virtual Reality*, *1*, 2-14. https://doi.org/10.3389/frvir.2020.576421

Sun, Y., Bao, Y., & Lu, L. (2020). Addressing mental health care for the bereaved during the COVID-19 pandemic. *Psychiatry and Clinical Neurosciences*, *74*(7), 406. https://doi.org/10.1111/pcn.13008

Wang, X., Gordon, R. M., & Snyder, E. W. (2021). Comparing Chinese and US practitioners' attitudes towards teletherapy during the COVID-19 pandemic. *Asia-Pacific Psychiatry*, *13*(1), 1-2. https://doi.org/10.1111/appy.12440

www.ingramcontent.com/pod-product-compliance
Lightning Source LLC
Chambersburg PA
CBHW020709270326
41928CB00005B/341

9 781773 696645